PRESENTATION

INTRODUCTION TO THE CONSULTING MARKET

FUNDAMENTALS OF CONSULTING SALES

DEFINING YOUR CONSULTING NICHE

BUILDING CREDIBILITY

DEVELOPING SERVICE OFFERINGS

PRICING TECHNIQUES IN CONSULTING

CONTENT MARKETING FOR CONSULTANTS

EFFECTIVE NETWORKING STRATEGIES

THE POWER OF REFERENCES

CONSULTATIVE SALES

NEGOTIATION IN CONSULTING

CUSTOMER RELATIONSHIP MANAGEMENT

USE OF CASE STUDY

ADAPTATION TO MARKET CHANGES

DIGITAL TOOLS FOR CONSULTANTS

DEVELOPMENT OF WINNING PROPOSALS

OVERCOMING SALES OBJECTIONS

CLOSE THE SALE

CULTURE AND INTERNATIONAL SALES

MEASURING SUCCESS IN CONSULTING SALES

TRAINING AND CONTINUOUS TRAINING

LEGISLATION AND ETHICS IN CONSULTING

SERVICE EXPANSION STRATEGIES

SUSTAINABILITY AND CONSULTING

FUTURE OF CONSULTING SALES

REGINALDO OSNILDO

Master Consulting Sales: Strategies for Converting Knowledge into Profit

Copyright © 2024 Reginaldo Osnildo
All rights reserved.

PRESENTATION

Welcome to the world of consulting sales, a challenging and extremely rewarding field. This book was specially developed for you, an individual consultant, consulting company or professional looking to not only improve your skills, but truly excel in transforming your technical and professional knowledge into tangible financial results. In " **Master Consulting Sales: Strategies for Converting Knowledge into Profit**", you'll find a detailed guide that will help you stand out in a competitive market by mastering the most effective sales and marketing strategies.

On every page, you'll discover that more than a compilation of information, this book is a conversation, a step-by-step guide, designed to be as practical as it is inspiring. My goal is to bring you an updated perspective on the most traditional concepts and integrate market innovations, facilitating your journey and optimizing your results.

You will learn to explore the current scenario in the consulting market, define your niche, build credibility, develop irresistible offers and pricing strategies that value your expertise. Additionally, we'll cover the power of content marketing, effective networking, the art of consultative selling, and how to manage lasting relationships with your customers.

This book is not just about theories; it is about practical application. You will be equipped with knowledge and tools to face real challenges, respond to sales objections efficiently, and close deals that not only satisfy but also exceed your customers' expectations. And at the end of each chapter, an invitation to continue the journey in the next one, ensuring continuous and engaged learning.

Are you ready to turn your knowledge into profit? Come, embark on this journey of learning and growth, and become a master of consultancy sales. In the next chapter, we'll begin by exploring the current landscape of the consulting market, the growing importance of these services, and how you can position yourself advantageously from the start. Let's go?

Yours sincerely

Reginaldo Osnildo

INTRODUCTION TO THE CONSULTING MARKET

The consulting market has evolved significantly over the years, becoming a crucial component for the success of companies of all sizes and sectors. Understanding this market is the first step for you, as you seek not only to participate, but to lead in this competitive field. This chapter offers an in-depth look at the current consulting landscape, highlighting its importance and how you can take advantage of emerging opportunities to establish and grow your consulting practice.

THE GROWTH OF THE CONSULTING MARKET

In recent years, the consulting market has seen robust growth, driven by the need for companies to adapt to rapid technological changes, complex regulations and increasing competitive pressures. Organizations of all types are seeking consultants not only for domain-specific insights, but also to gain strategic advantages that only an outside, expert view can provide.

WHY IS CONSULTING MORE IMPORTANT NOW?

In the current context, consultancy is more than a service; it is a strategic necessity. Companies face multifaceted challenges that require equally complex and customized solutions. You, as a consultant, have the unique opportunity to act as a catalyst for innovation and transformation within these organizations.

UNDERSTANDING MARKET NEEDS

To be effective in consultancy sales, it is crucial to deeply understand market needs. This includes knowing the sectors most likely to seek advice, such as technology, healthcare, finance and education, and understanding the specific problems these sectors face. Such insights allow you to develop tailored solutions that directly resonate with your prospects' challenges.

POSITIONING YOURSELF FOR SUCCESS

Success in the consulting market begins with strategic positioning. Identifying and understanding market trends such as digitalization, sustainability and service personalization can help you align your consultancy offering with future demands. Additionally, being aware of economic and regulatory fluctuations can empower you to adapt your strategies proactively.

This overview of the consulting market is intended to be your starting point. With this understanding, you are better equipped to navigate this complex and opportunity-filled environment. The knowledge gained here will be the foundation on which we will build effective sales strategies in the next chapters.

As we move into the next chapter, we will dive into the " **FUNDAMENTALS OF CONSULTING SALES** ." You will learn the key elements that differentiate consulting sales from other types of sales, and how this knowledge can be applied to maximize your effectiveness and profitability. Are you ready to continue this journey? Let's explore together the pillars of effective consulting sales.

FUNDAMENTALS OF CONSULTING SALES

Selling consulting services is an art that combines profound technical understanding with exceptional interactive skills. This chapter will focus on the key elements that differentiate consultancy sales from other forms of sales, showing how you can apply these principles to effectively convert your knowledge into profit.

UNDERSTANDING THE NATURE OF CONSULTING

Unlike standardized products or services, consulting is highly personalized and relationship-based. Each client has unique needs, which requires you, as a consultant, to have an adaptive and consultative approach. This means listening carefully, understanding the customer's specific pain points and then proposing solutions that perfectly align with their requirements.

CONSULTANCY AS A SALE OF SOLUTIONS

The heart of consulting sales is positioning yourself as a problem solver. You are not just selling a service, but offering a promise of transformation and improvement. It is essential to demonstrate how your expertise can solve specific problems, optimize processes and improve your client's overall efficiency.

BUILDING LONG-TERM RELATIONSHIPS

Consulting sales are rarely one-time transactions; they involve the development of long-term relationships. Trust is a critical component here. Investing time in getting to know your client, understanding their business culture and long-term goals can transform an initial contract into a lasting partnership.

DEMONSTRATING VALUE EARLY

An effective strategy in consultancy sales is demonstrating value even before the purchase. This can be accomplished through workshops, seminars, quality content or free preliminary consultations. Such initiatives help establish your credibility and solidify your position as the preferred choice when a client decides to move forward.

COMMUNICATING EFFECTIVELY

Communication is vital in any sale, but in consultancy sales, it is especially critical. You need to be able to clearly articulate how your consultancy can benefit the client in a quantifiable way. This often involves translating complex concepts into clear, accessible language, ensuring the customer fully understands the potential impact and value of your offering.

Mastering the fundamentals of consulting sales puts you in a prime position to make the most of your skills and knowledge. By understanding the unique nature of this type of selling, you will be better equipped to connect with your customers and create proposals that truly respond to their needs.

In the next chapter, " **DEFINING YOUR CONSULTING NICHE** ," we will explore how to identify and choose a niche market that is not only profitable but also perfectly aligned with your knowledge and passions. Ready to delve even deeper and find your ideal space in the consulting market? Let's go!

DEFINING YOUR CONSULTING NICHE

Identifying and choosing the correct niche is crucial to the success of any consultant. This chapter will guide you through the process of defining a profitable niche market that aligns with your knowledge and experience. By focusing on a specific niche, you not only increase your chances of success, but you also position yourself as an expert, which is vital in a competitive market.

THE IMPORTANCE OF CHOOSING THE RIGHT NICHE

In consulting, being perceived as an expert can significantly impact your ability to attract and retain clients. A well-defined niche allows you to stand out, reduces competition and increases the relevance of your offering to a specific group of potential customers. Furthermore, it makes it easier to customize your marketing and sales strategies for a more defined and accessible audience.

STEPS TO IDENTIFY YOUR IDEAL NICHE

1. **Assess your passion and expertise:** Start with what you know and love. Passion for your work not only keeps you motivated but is also contagious to your clients.
2. **Market research:** Examine which sectors or types of companies can benefit most from your consultancy. Look at market trends, growing demands and underserved areas.
3. **Market validation:** Check if there is a real demand for the services you intend to offer. This can be done through interviews with potential customers, competitor analysis and peer feedback.
4. **Specialize:** After choosing a market segment, dig even deeper. For example, instead of just "financial consulting," consider "financial consulting for tech startups."
5. **Test and adjust:** Initially launch small test services or offerings to gauge market response. Use the feedback to refine your offer.

COMMUNICATING YOUR NICHE

Once you've defined your niche, it's essential that you clearly communicate this focus across all of your marketing channels and customer touchpoints. This includes your website, social media profiles, marketing materials, and especially your sales proposal.

Defining and mastering your consulting niche is not just about finding a place in the market, but creating a space in which you are seen as the undisputed authority. This not only increases the effectiveness of your sales but also contributes to building a sustainable and profitable consulting practice.

Are you ready to build your authority and credibility within your chosen niche? In the next chapter, " **BUILDING CREDIBILITY** ", we will explore effective tactics for establishing your authority and increasing your visibility in the market. These strategies will be key to transforming your technical knowledge into a profitable consulting practice. Let's go on this journey together?

BUILDING CREDIBILITY

Credibility is the foundation on which a successful career in consulting is built. This chapter will guide you on how to establish and reinforce your authority and credibility in the niche you have chosen. Let's explore practical tactics you can implement to be recognized as a trusted expert, attracting more clients and consolidating your position in the market.

WHY IS CREDIBILITY CRUCIAL?

In the world of consulting, trust is an essential component. Your potential clients must believe in your ability to deliver results before they even hire you. A solid, credible reputation not only makes it easier to acquire new clients, it also increases loyalty among existing clients, resulting in more referrals and a thriving consulting practice.

ESTABLISHING YOUR AUTHORITY

1. **Education and certifications:** Continue investing in your education. Recognized certifications in your area of specialization can add invaluable value to your profile.
2. **Publications:** Write articles, case studies, or books about your area of expertise. Being published in respected journals or online platforms establishes you as an authoritative voice in the field.
3. **Speaking and workshops:** Offer to speak at conferences, workshops or webinars. These are great spaces to showcase your knowledge and connect directly with potential clients.
4. **Using testimonials:** Collect and use testimonials from previous customers. The words of a satisfied customer are one of the best ways to prove your competence and results.
5. **Strategic partnerships:** Align with other companies or consultants that can complement your service offering. Well-chosen partnerships can increase your visibility

and accessibility.

BUILDING VISIBILITY

Staying visible is just as important as building your authority. Use all the tools available to keep your name in the minds of potential customers:

- **Social media:** Maintain an active presence on the social media platforms where your prospects spend their time. Share relevant content that highlights your expertise.
- **SEO (Search engine Optimization):** Optimize your website content to ensure it appears in search results when potential clients search for consultants in their area.
- **Networking:** Continue expanding your network of contacts. The more people know you and your work, the greater your credibility in the market.

Building and maintaining credibility requires continuous effort and consistency. Every interaction you have in the marketplace is an opportunity to solidify your reputation as a trustworthy and capable advisor.

Ready to take the next step and start structuring your service offerings in a way that maximizes the value perceived by your customers? In the next chapter, " **DEVELOPING SERVICE OFFERINGS** ", we will explore how you can create offerings that not only meet your customers' needs but also exceed their expectations, thus ensuring their satisfaction and business continuity. Let's continue this journey together?

DEVELOPING SERVICE OFFERINGS

Creating service offerings that not only meet but also exceed client expectations is one of the most crucial aspects for any consultant. In this chapter, we will explore how to structure your offerings to maximize the value perceived by clients, ensuring the relevance and effectiveness of your services in the competitive consulting market.

UNDERSTANDING CUSTOMER NEEDS

Before developing your offers, it is essential to deeply understand your customers' needs and challenges. This can be achieved through:

- **Open dialogue:** Conduct interviews or brainstorming sessions with potential customers to understand their problems and expectations.
- **Market research:** Utilize market data and feedback from past customers to identify emerging trends and needs.
- **Competitor analysis:** Observe how other consultants are meeting (or failing to meet) market needs and find spaces to innovate.

STRUCTURING YOUR OFFERS

1. **Service packages:** Create service packages that group complementary solutions. This not only simplifies the purchasing decision for the customer, but also increases its perceived value.
2. **Personalization:** Offer options to personalize services according to the customer's specific needs. Customization can be a great competitive differentiator.
3. **Flexible pricing models:** Develop pricing structures that adapt to different client budgets and project sizes. This may include flat fees, value-based pricing, or retention models.
4. **Service guarantees:** Consider offering some type of guarantee that assures the customer about the quality and effectiveness of the services provided.

Maximizing Perceived Value

- **Demonstration of ROI (Return on Investment):** Get ready to show how your services provide a clear and measurable return. This can be done through case studies, past service performance data and testimonials from satisfied customers.
- **Clear Communication of Benefits:** Make sure your proposals and marketing materials clearly articulate the benefits of your offerings. Use language that resonates with the client's specific industry and highlights tangible results.
- **Continuous updates and improvements:** Show customers that your offerings are always evolving based on new market trends and feedback. This reinforces the long-term value of working with you.

Developing well-structured service offerings is essential to creating and maintaining a successful consulting practice. By focusing on your customers' needs and maximizing perceived value, you not only meet their expectations, but exceed them, ensuring a lasting and profitable relationship.

Ready to explore even more about how to strategically set up your pricing? In the next chapter, " **PRICING TECHNIQUES IN CONSULTING**", we'll dive into strategies for setting prices that reflect your value and expertise, without discouraging potential clients. Let's move forward on this journey together?

PRICING TECHNIQUES IN CONSULTING

Setting the right pricing strategy is vital to the success of your consulting practice. This chapter discusses how to set prices that appropriately reflect your value and expertise, while remaining competitive and affordable for your potential customers. Let's explore different pricing techniques and how to apply them effectively in your consulting business.

UNDERSTANDING VALUE-BASED PRICING

One of the most effective approaches in consulting is value-based pricing. This method goes beyond simply calculating hours worked, focusing on the value that your service adds to the customer. To implement this strategy, it is crucial:

- **Identify perceived value:** Understand how your customers value your services. This can vary significantly depending on the industry and specific customer needs.
- **Communicate value:** Ensure customers clearly understand the return they can expect on their investment. This can be done through presentations, detailed proposals and case studies that demonstrate the positive impact of your previous services.

COMMON PRICING MODELS IN CONSULTING

1. **Pricing per project:** Price a complete project based on the scope of work and expected results. This approach is ideal for projects with clear and defined objectives.
2. **Hourly price:** Billing based on the time dedicated to the project. Although it is simple, it may not adequately reflect the value delivered, especially in projects that require a high level of specialization.
3. **Monthly Retainer:** A fixed monthly fee for services over an established period. This provides predictable revenue and builds long-term customer relationships.
4. **Results-based:** Pricing that depends on the achievement of certain results or goals. This model can

be very attractive to clients as it reduces perceived risk.

STRATEGIES FOR SETTING COMPETITIVE PRICES

- **Market analysis:** Stay informed about how your competitors are pricing similar services. This helps ensure your prices are in line with the market, while still highlighting the additional value you offer.
- **Flexibility:** Be open to negotiating with clients, especially on long-term contracts or large-scale projects where customized pricing may be more appropriate.
- **Periodic reviews:** Evaluate and adjust your prices regularly to reflect changes in the market, your service offering and your own experience and reputation.

Pricing is more than just a number; it's a communication of the value your service provides. A well-thought-out pricing strategy not only guarantees profitability, but also reinforces the perception of value of your work among customers.

Ready to dive into how to effectively use content marketing to attract and engage potential customers? In the next chapter, " **CONTENT MARKETING FOR CONSULTANTS** ," we'll explore techniques for using educational content that not only informs but also engages your target audience, strengthening your brand and expanding your customer base. Let's continue this journey together?

CONTENT MARKETING FOR CONSULTANTS

In the competitive consulting market, content marketing emerges as a powerful tool for attracting and engaging potential clients, establishing your authority and differentiating your brand. This chapter will explore how you can effectively use educational content to build a solid market presence, capture the interest of your target audience, and create a steady flow of qualified leads.

WHY IS CONTENT MARKETING ESSENTIAL FOR CONSULTANTS?

Content marketing allows you to share your knowledge and expertise without the need for direct sales, which can help build trust and respect with your audience. It offers a platform to demonstrate your competence and insights, while solving your potential clients' queries and problems, positioning you as the ideal choice when they need consultancy.

EFFECTIVE CONTENT TYPES FOR CONSULTANTS

1. **Blogs and articles:** Regular posts on your website can improve your SEO, helping more customers find you online. Write about topics that resonate with your areas of expertise and the needs of your audience.
2. **E-books and guides:** Offer deeper resources, such as e-books or how-to guides, that can be used as lead generation tools. Ask your website visitors to provide their email in exchange for access to material, thus building your contact list.
3. **Videos:** Create explainer videos or webinars that discuss complex topics in an accessible way. Videos are highly engaging and can significantly increase the time visitors spend on your website.
4. **Case studies:** Demonstrate how you solved specific problems for previous clients through detailed case studies. These are particularly effective at showcasing your process and results, serving as social proof of your effectiveness.

5. **Newsletters:** Keep your audience informed and engaged with regular updates about your area of expertise, new services, and industry insights, directly in their emails.

STRATEGIES TO MAXIMIZE THE IMPACT OF YOUR CONTENT

- **Define your target audience:** Understand who your ideal customers are and what they need. This will help you create content that speaks directly to their concerns and needs.
- **Utilize SEO:** Optimize your content for search engines to improve your online visibility. Relevant keywords, attractive titles and quality content are key.
- **Cross-promotion on social platforms:** Share your content on social media platforms where your audience spends time. This not only increases the reach of your content but also drives traffic to your website.
- **Analysis and tuning:** Use analytical tools to monitor the performance of your content. See what resonates with your audience and adjust your strategy as needed to improve results.

Content marketing is a crucial strategic tool for any consultant looking to establish a strong brand and generate qualified leads. By investing in quality content that educates and engages, you not only build credibility but also establish a lasting connection with your audience.

Ready to expand your network and harness the power of networking? In the next chapter, " **EFFECTIVE NETWORKING STRATEGIES** ," we will explore valuable techniques for using networking to generate leads and business opportunities. Continue on this journey to further strengthen your consulting practice. Let's go ahead?

EFFECTIVE NETWORKING STRATEGIES

Networking is an essential skill for any consultant, as it opens doors to new business opportunities, strengthens professional relationships and builds a robust reputation in the market. In this chapter, we'll explore effective networking strategies that can help you genuinely connect with colleagues, potential clients, and influencers in your field.

THE IMPORTANCE OF NETWORKING IN CONSULTING

Effective networking allows you to access resources, knowledge and opportunities that might otherwise be inaccessible. It offers a two-way street: you gain insights and support, while providing value and knowledge to others. Additionally, a solid network can be an ongoing source of referrals and new business.

IDENTIFYING NETWORKING OPPORTUNITIES

1. **Industry Events:** Regularly attend conferences, seminars and workshops related to your consulting field. These events are ideal places to meet thought leaders and potential customers.
2. **Professional groups:** Join professional groups and organizations where you can find other like-minded consultants and business professionals. Actively participating can increase your visibility and establish your reputation as a valued member of the community.
3. **Online networking platforms:** Use platforms like LinkedIn to build and maintain professional contacts. Share relevant content, participate in discussions, and connect with new people regularly.
4. **Local Networking:** Don't underestimate the power of local networking. Attending local chamber of commerce events and other business gatherings can open doors and connect you with business leaders in your area.

BEST PRACTICES FOR EFFECTIVE NETWORKING

- **Be proactive:** Don't wait for opportunities to come to you. Be the initiator of conversations and collaborative projects.
- **Listen more than you talk:** Showing genuine interest in other people's stories and challenges can help build stronger, more memorable relationships.
- **Offer value:** Before you ask someone for something, think about how you can offer value first. This could be in the form of a useful resource, a valuable introduction or practical advice.
- **Stay in touch:** Effective networking doesn't end after the first meeting. Follow up regularly and stay top of people's minds. This could be through email messages, follow-up calls, or even a simple social media post.

Networking is not just about collecting as many contacts as possible; It's about creating meaningful relationships that can generate long-term mutual benefits. Invest time and energy in developing your network and reap the rewards of a more connected and successful consulting career.

Ready to turn these contacts into customers? In the next chapter, " **THE POWER OF REFERRALS** ," we'll explore how to cultivate and leverage referrals to boost sales and grow your consulting practice. Let's move forward on this journey of growth together?

THE POWER OF REFERENCES

Referrals are one of the most effective and reliable ways to generate new business for consultants. This chapter covers how you can cultivate and leverage referrals to not only boost your sales, but also solidify customer trust and loyalty. We will explore strategies to motivate customers to share their positive experience with others, turning every satisfied customer into an active promoter of your services.

THE IMPORTANCE OF REFERENCES IN CONSULTING

Referrals generate a virtuous cycle of new business with significantly lower acquisition costs and higher conversion rates than other marketing channels. A client who comes to you through a referral is already pre-selected and has an established level of trust, based on a recommendation from someone they respect.

BUILDING AN EFFECTIVE REFERRAL STRATEGY

1. **Service Excellence:** The basis for receiving referrals is the consistent delivery of exceptional service. Satisfied customers are naturally more likely to speak positively about their experience.
2. **Actively ask for referrals:** Don't assume clients will offer referrals without being asked. Find the right time to ask for references, usually after the successful delivery of a project or when the client expresses satisfaction.
3. **Make the referral process easier:** Provide your customers with tools that make referrals easier, like links to your contact page, explanatory materials, or even a simple form they can send to their friends.
4. **Recognize and reward referrals:** Show appreciation for referrals through thanks, bonuses or discounts. This not only gratifies the referring customer, but also encourages similar future behavior.

EXAMPLES OF HOW TO TAKE ADVANTAGE OF REFERENCES

- **Testimonials and case studies:** Use customer testimonials and in-depth case studies in your marketing. Showcasing real success stories increases your credibility and shows the tangible impact of your work.
- **Referral programs:** Implement a formal referral program that offers incentives for both the new customer and the person who referred you. Make sure the benefits are attractive and relevant to both of you.
- **Continued Networking:** Stay in touch with past clients. Periodically remind them of your work and how you can help your contacts.

Referrals are a powerful force in the consulting world, capable of significantly boosting the growth of your business. By investing in quality relationships and implementing a structured referral strategy, you maximize your chances of attracting new, highly qualified clients.

Ready to apply what you've learned about referrals to your consultative sales practice? In the next chapter, " **CONSULTATIVE SALES** ", we'll explore specific sales techniques that focus on understanding and solving customer problems, further solidifying trust and expanding your consulting success. Let's move forward on this successful journey together?

CONSULTATIVE SALES

Consultative selling is a powerful method for consultants, as it focuses on understanding and solving customer needs in a personalized and in-depth way. This chapter explores how you can apply consultative selling techniques to enhance customer interactions and maximize your chances of success. Consultative selling is not just about selling a service, but about establishing a relationship of trust and partnership.

UNDERSTANDING CONSULTATIVE SALES

Consultative selling is based on the idea that the salesperson acts more like a trusted advisor than a traditional salesperson. This method requires an in-depth understanding of the client's needs, challenges, and goals. The goal is to create solutions that not only solve immediate problems but also promote long-term customer success.

FUNDAMENTAL STEPS OF CONSULTATIVE SALES

1. **Research and preparation:** Before meeting with the client, do detailed research about their company, industry and competition. This shows that you are knowledgeable and serious about helping.
2. **Active listening:** During client meetings, practice active listening. Understand not only what is said, but also what is not directly expressed. This helps to truly identify customer needs.
3. **Problem Diagnosis:** Use the information collected to diagnose problems (some of which the customer may not be aware of). Present these problems clearly, based on data and concrete examples.
4. **Customized solutions:** Offer solutions that are directly aligned with the customer's needs and objectives. Personalize your proposals to show how you can meet their specific needs.
5. **Collaborative closing:** Invest in closing the sale as a collaborative process, where you and the customer work

together to adjust and refine the proposed solution until it completely meets the customer's needs.

BUILDING CREDIBILITY AND TRUST

- **Provide evidence:** Use case studies, testimonials and performance data to support your recommendations. Tangible evidence increases your credibility.
- **Be transparent:** Be honest about what your consultancy can and cannot do. Transparency is vital to building trust.
- **Follow-up:** After the sale, maintain contact with the customer to ensure the solutions are working as expected. This shows commitment to long-term customer success.

Adhering to the consultative sales model can transform the way you interact with clients, taking your consulting practice to new levels of professionalism and effectiveness. This method allows you to position yourself as a true partner to the client, contributing significantly to their success.

Ready to deepen your skills in negotiating effectively? In the next chapter, " **NEGOTIATION IN CONSULTING**", we will explore methods for negotiating contracts that are beneficial to both parties. We will continue to enrich your consulting techniques with a focus on exceptional results. Let's go together?

NEGOTIATION IN CONSULTING

Negotiation is an essential skill for consultants, who often face the challenge of aligning their value propositions with clients' expectations and budgets. This chapter will help you develop effective methods for negotiating consulting contracts, ensuring that both you and your clients leave satisfied and committed to mutual success.

UNDERSTANDING THE DYNAMICS OF NEGOTIATION

Negotiating is not just about reaching an agreement on price. It is a complex process that involves discussing terms of service, project scope, schedules and, sometimes, after-sales guarantees. Good negotiation should aim for an agreement that benefits both parties, creating a lasting partnership based on mutual respect and trust.

NEGOTIATION STRATEGIES FOR CONSULTANTS

1. **Preparation and research:** Before entering into a negotiation, prepare yourself meticulously. Understand the customer's needs, their pressure points and their budget. Have a clear understanding of your own limits and goals.
2. **Build relationships:** Begin the negotiation by establishing a positive relationship. Showing empathy and genuine interest can create a favorable atmosphere for open dialogue.
3. **Clearly communicate your value:** Make sure the customer understands the value you are bringing. Reinforce how your solutions can solve their problems or improve their current situation.
4. **Be flexible but firm:** Be open to different configurations and solutions, but be firm on the points that are crucial to the viability of your service. Know when and where to make concessions without compromising the quality and integrity of your work.
5. **Strategic closing:** Know how to recognize the right

moment to close the negotiation. Once all parties are reasonably satisfied, summarize the agreed terms to avoid future misunderstandings and solidify the commitment.

TACTICS FOR DEALING WITH OBJECTIONS

- **Anticipate common objections:** Prepare with answers to potential objections clients may raise about costs, scope, or duration of services.
- **Use the "Yes, and..." technique:** When faced with an objection, validate it ("yes") and add information that might alleviate the concern ("and..."), showing how you can adjust the offer to meet customer needs.
- **Turn objections into opportunities:** See each objection as a chance to better understand the customer and refine your proposal to better meet their needs.

The ability to negotiate effectively is crucial to success in consulting. By applying the strategies discussed, you will be able to conduct negotiations that not only result in profitable contracts, but also build the foundation for long-lasting and productive relationships with your clients.

Ready to explore how to maintain and nurture these relationships over the long term? In the next chapter, " **CUSTOMER RELATIONSHIP MANAGEMENT** ," we will discuss strategies for developing and maintaining long-term relationships with your clients, which are the backbone of any successful consulting practice. Let's move forward on this journey together?

CUSTOMER RELATIONSHIP MANAGEMENT

Long-term success in consulting depends heavily on maintaining and cultivating lasting client relationships. This chapter explores effective strategies for managing these relationships, ensuring that you not only meet customer expectations, but also exceed them, fostering an environment of trust and ongoing collaboration.

THE IMPORTANCE OF LONG-LASTING RELATIONSHIPS

Long-term relationships with clients bring mutual benefits: for the client, continuity allows for a more personalized service that evolves with their needs; For the consultant, stable relationships generate predictable revenue streams and new business opportunities through referrals.

BUILDING STRONG RELATIONSHIPS

1. **Regular and open communication:** Maintaining open lines of communication is crucial. This includes regular updates on project progress and discussions about changes to the client's needs or objectives.
2. **Deep understanding of customer needs:** Dig deeper into your customers' business goals and the forces driving their market. The more you understand their challenges and goals, the better you will be able to serve them.
3. **Quick response to issues:** Be quick and efficient in resolving any issues or concerns that arise. This shows the customer that you are committed to service quality and satisfaction.
4. **Anticipating needs:** Don't wait for customers to come to you with all their problems. Be proactive, anticipating needs they may have in the future and suggesting solutions even before they become an urgent concern.

STRATEGIES TO IMPROVE CUSTOMER RETENTION

- **Service customization:** Tailor your services to meet

each client's specific needs. A personalized approach increases the relevance and perceived value of your work.
- **Value-added offerings:** Consider offering additional services that complement the work you already do for the client, such as training sessions, educational webinars, or periodic performance reviews.
- **Loyalty programs:** Implement programs that reward long-time customers for their loyalty. This could include discounts, exclusive services or access to special events.

USING FEEDBACK TO IMPROVE SERVICE

- **Actively solicit feedback:** Encourage clients to share their impressions of your work. Not only does this provide valuable information to improve your services, but it also makes customers feel valued and heard.
- **Feedback analysis and implementation:** Use the feedback you receive to make concrete adjustments to your services. Demonstrating that you are willing to evolve based on customer input can significantly strengthen their trust and loyalty.

Managing customer relationships is an art that requires dedication, empathy and a proactive approach. Investing in solid, long-lasting relationships is not just good business practice; is an essential strategy for ensuring sustainable growth and client satisfaction in your consulting practice.

Ready to further demonstrate your value and success through case studies? In the next chapter, " **USE OF CASE STUDY** ", we will explore how you can use case studies to not only prove your competence and success, but also to capture the imagination of potential clients. Shall we continue to deepen your skills and knowledge?

USE OF CASE STUDY

Case studies are extremely powerful tools for demonstrating the effectiveness of your consulting services. Not only do they highlight your skills and past successes, they also provide a compelling narrative that potential clients can visualize and relate to their own needs. This chapter will cover how you can effectively use case studies to bolster your credibility and attract more customers.

WHY USE CASE STUDY?

Case studies serve as concrete proof of your success and ability to solve complex problems. They transform abstract concepts into tangible results and allow potential clients to see how you applied your knowledge and skills in real situations. Additionally, they can be used to educate clients about the consulting process and expected results.

CREATING EFFECTIVE CASE STUDY

1. **Project selection:** Choose projects that represent your area of expertise well and that have clear success stories. It's important that the cases you select resonate with the type of client you want to attract.
2. **Case study structure:** An effective case study should contain:
    - **Context:** Describe the client, the problem they faced and why they chose your consultancy.
    - **Process:** Explain how you approached the problem, the strategies you used, and any challenges you faced.
    - **Results:** Highlight the concrete results obtained and how they benefited the client.
    - **Testimonials:** Including quotes or customer testimonials adds a layer of authenticity and emotion.
3. **Visuals and data:** Use graphs, tables, and other visual representations to make the data more accessible and

the story more compelling.

DISCLOSING YOUR CASE STUDY

- **Website and marketing materials:** Post your case studies on your website, create brochures or ebooks that customers can download. This not only increases your visibility but also serves as reference material for interested customers.
- **Social media and blogs:** Share your case studies on social media and write blog posts that detail specific aspects of the cases. This can generate discussions and attract attention to your expertise.
- **Proposals and presentations:** Include relevant case studies in your proposals and presentations to new clients. They are compelling evidence of your past success and can help close new deals.

EVALUATING THE IMPACT OF CASE STUDY

- **Client feedback:** Solicit feedback from clients on how the case studies influenced their decision to engage your services.
- **Performance analysis:** Monitor traffic and interaction with case studies on your website and social media. Use this data to adjust your approach and improve content.

Case studies are powerful narratives that prove your ability to generate meaningful and lasting results for your clients. They not only increase your credibility, but are also key in convincing potential customers of the real value you can add to their business.

Ready to adjust your approach to market changes? In the next chapter, " **ADAPTATION TO MARKET CHANGES** ," we'll explore tactics for keeping your consulting practice relevant and effective in an ever-changing business environment. Let's move forward to ensure you remain at the forefront of consulting?

ADAPTATION TO MARKET CHANGES

The ability to adapt to changes in the market is crucial to keeping your consulting practice relevant and effective. In this chapter, we'll explore strategies for adjusting your approach in response to emerging trends and industry developments, ensuring you continue to deliver meaningful value to your customers even in uncertain times.

UNDERSTANDING MARKET DYNAMICS

The first step to adapting to market changes is understanding the forces that shape those changes. This includes being aware of economic trends, technological developments, new regulations and changing consumer expectations. Staying informed through ongoing research and market analysis is critical.

ADAPTATION STRATEGIES

1. **Flexibility in services offered:** Be ready to adjust your service offering to meet changing customer needs. This may include introducing new services, discontinuing less relevant ones, or modifying delivery methods.
2. **Continuous training:** Invest in your own education and that of your team. Attending courses, workshops and seminars on the latest industry trends not only broadens your skills but also demonstrates your commitment to excellence.
3. **Technology and innovation:** Adopt new technologies that can improve the efficiency and effectiveness of your services. Digital tools can help optimize internal processes and the customer experience, as well as open new communication and marketing channels.
4. **Strategic partnerships:** Forming alliances with other companies can offer new insights and resources that help you adapt your services to market needs. These partnerships can also expand your market reach and customer base.
5. **Customer feedback:** Encourage and value regular

customer feedback. Understanding their experiences and expectations can provide valuable insights into how to better tailor your services.

IMPLEMENTING CHANGES

- **Careful planning:** Before implementing any changes, plan carefully to minimize disruption and ensure a smooth transition for customers.
- **Clear communication:** Communicate any changes clearly and effectively to all stakeholders. Explain the reasons for the changes and the expected benefits for customers.
- **Monitoring and adjusting:** After implementing changes, monitor the impact of these changes on your business and adjust as necessary to optimize results and customer satisfaction.

Adapting to market changes is not just a necessity; It is an opportunity to innovate and grow. By remaining agile and responsive to industry trends and customer needs, you can not only survive in an ever-changing business environment, but also thrive.

Ready to explore digital tools that can optimize your sales and service delivery? In the next chapter, " **DIGITAL TOOLS FOR CONSULTANTS** ," we'll dive into the technologies that are transforming the consulting industry and how you can use them to enhance your practice. Will we continue to be at the forefront of innovation?

DIGITAL TOOLS FOR CONSULTANTS

The adoption of digital tools is essential for consultants who want to optimize their operations and improve service delivery. This chapter explores several technologies that can transform the way you interact with clients, manage projects, and market your services, delivering greater efficiency and better results.

THE IMPORTANCE OF DIGITAL TOOLS

In an increasingly digital market, technological tools are not just facilitators; they are differentiators. They allow consultants to stand out for their efficiency, quality of service and ability to respond quickly to client needs.

TYPES OF DIGITAL TOOLS FOR CONSULTANTS

1. **CRM (Customer Relationship Management):** CRM systems help manage and analyze interactions with customers throughout the entire relationship cycle. They make it easy to track leads, manage contacts, run marketing campaigns, and provide personalized services.
2. **Collaboration and communication platforms:** Tools like Slack, Microsoft Teams, and Zoom enable real-time communication and collaboration with teams and clients, regardless of geographic location.
3. **Project management tools:** Software like Asana, Trello and Monday.com help you plan, organize and track projects efficiently. They are essential for maintaining deadlines, delegating tasks and monitoring progress.
4. **Data analysis software:** Data analysis and visualization tools, such as Tableau and Google Analytics, are crucial for extracting insights from large volumes of data, allowing you to make evidence-based recommendations.
5. **Marketing automation:** Platforms like HubSpot and Mailchimp automate repetitive marketing tasks such as email marketing, social media marketing and lead

generation, increasing the efficiency and effectiveness of campaigns.

IMPLEMENTING DIGITAL TOOLS

- **Needs assessment:** Determine which processes could be improved with technology. Consider your specific business needs and the needs of your customers.
- **Choice of tools:** Select tools that best align with your needs and that easily integrate with other technologies already in use.
- **Training and adoption:** Train your team to use new tools efficiently. Successful adoption often depends on a clear understanding of how tools contribute to business objectives.
- **Continuous assessment:** Monitor the impact of tools on your business and make adjustments as needed. Be open to trying new technologies as they emerge.

Digital tools offer a variety of benefits, from improving operational efficiency to optimizing the customer experience. By integrating the right technology into your consulting practice, you can not only increase your productivity but also provide a higher quality service that stands out in the competitive market.

Ready for the next step? In the next chapter, " **DEVELOPMENT OF WINNING PROPOSALS** ", we will discuss how to create proposals that not only capture customers' attention, but also convince them to choose your services. Let's move forward to ensure your proposals are as effective as possible?

DEVELOPMENT OF WINNING PROPOSALS

Creating winning proposals is an essential skill for consultants, as it is through them that you present your competence, understand the client's needs and propose solutions that resonate in a convincing way. This chapter offers detailed guidance on how to structure proposals that not only stand out but also persuade clients to choose your services.

THE IMPORTANCE OF A WELL PREPARED PROPOSAL

An effective proposal should do more than just describe the services you offer. It must connect with the customer on a level that addresses their specific problems, presents clear solutions, and demonstrates the value you can bring to their organization. The proposal is often the first decisive step towards establishing a lasting relationship with the client.

ELEMENTS OF A WINNING PROPOSAL

1. **Clear understanding of the client's needs:** Before you start writing your proposal, make sure you have a deep understanding of the client's needs and challenges. This can be achieved through initial meetings, questionnaires or analysis of briefs provided by the client.
2. **Well-defined objectives and targets:** Clearly specify how the proposed services will help the client achieve their objectives. This includes setting specific, measurable and time-bound goals.
3. **Detailed description of services:** Provide a detailed explanation of each service you are proposing, how it will be performed, and why it is the best solution for the customer.
4. **Demonstration of value and ROI:** Highlight the return on investment the customer can expect. Use data, statistics or case studies to substantiate your claims and show the effectiveness of your solutions.
5. **Realistic timeline:** Include a timeline for project

execution, showing key phases and milestones. This conveys organization and the ability to deliver results within a stipulated deadline.
6. **Transparent cost structure:** Present a clear cost structure that details how prices are calculated. Being transparent about costs helps build trust and avoids future misunderstandings.
7. **Clear terms and conditions:** Specify the terms and conditions of the proposal, including any warranty or after-sales support you offer.

TIPS TO MAKE YOUR PROPOSAL MORE ATTRACTIVE

- **Personalization:** Customize each proposal to reflect the client's brand and culture. This shows that you're not just recycling a generic proposal, but that you've invested the time to create something specific to them.
- **Readability:** Use headings, bullet lists, and graphics to make the proposal visually pleasing and easy to read. Dense texts can discourage the client from reading the proposal completely.
- **Call to action:** Include a clear call to action at the end of the proposal. Encourage the client to contact you to discuss the proposal in more detail or to take the next step in the process.

A well-crafted proposal is the key to converting opportunities into effective contracts. By applying the guidelines and techniques outlined, you will be well equipped to create proposals that not only capture clients' attention, but also convince them that you are the right choice for their consulting needs.

Ready to deal with the most common objections that may arise during the sales process? In the next chapter, " **OVERCOMING SALES OBJECTIONS** ," we'll explore effective techniques for responding to objections and ensuring you can maintain productive, progressive dialogue with your prospects. Let's continue improving your consulting skills?

OVERCOMING SALES OBJECTIONS

Overcoming objections is a crucial part of the consulting sales process. Each objection is an opportunity to better understand the customer's concerns and reaffirm the value of your services. This chapter discusses techniques for effectively handling common objections, turning potential barriers into compelling reasons to move forward with your proposal.

UNDERSTANDING SALES OBJECTIONS

Objections in sales often arise from doubts or concerns that the customer has about investing in your services. They may be related to cost, the suitability of the service to the customer's needs, confidence in the ability to deliver results, or the urgency of the purchase. Identifying the root of objections is the first step to being able to respond to them effectively.

STRATEGIES TO OVERCOME OBJECTIONS

1. **Active listening:** Listen carefully to what the customer is saying without interrupting. Often, the way an objection is expressed can provide insight into your true concerns.
2. **Clarify the objection:** Make sure you correctly understand the objection by asking clarifying questions. This shows the customer that you are genuinely interested in resolving their concerns.
3. **Reframe the objection as a need:** Turn the objection into an expression of a need or concern the customer has, and then demonstrate how your service can meet that need.
4. **Provide evidence:** Use data, case studies, or testimonials to validate your claims. Showing evidence of past success can reduce anxiety and build credibility.
5. **Offer alternative solutions:** If the objection cannot be completely overcome, offer alternative solutions or adjustments to your service that can address the customer's concerns.

COMMON TECHNIQUES FOR DEALING WITH SPECIFIC OBJECTIONS

- **Cost:** If cost is the main concern, justify the price with the return on investment (ROI) the customer can expect. Discuss how your service can save money in the long run or contribute to business growth.
- **Timing:** If the customer does not feel urgency, emphasize the importance of acting quickly due to market conditions or opportunities that may be missed.
- **Reliability:** If there are doubts about the ability to deliver results, reference previous clients who have had success with similar services. Offer reassurance if appropriate.
- **Fit:** If the customer is concerned about the fit of the service, discuss how you can customize your approach to meet their exact needs.

Overcoming objections is not just about answering questions, but about reinforcing the trust relationship and showing your commitment to achieving the best result for the client. By adopting these techniques, you will transform doubts into constructive dialogue and pave the way for closing more sales.

Ready to learn how to complete these negotiations successfully? In the next chapter, " **CLOSING THE SALE** ," we will explore strategies for converting these discussions into signed contracts, thus solidifying the transition from prospects to active customers. Let's continue to improve your sales skills?

CLOSE THE SALE

Closing the sale is the critical moment when all your interactions and efforts with the customer converge on a final decision. This chapter offers effective strategies for you to convert negotiations into signed contracts, ensuring that your sales efforts culminate in success.

UNDERSTANDING THE MOMENT OF CLOSING

Identifying the right time to close the sale is essential. This moment usually comes when you have addressed all of the client's objections, clearly demonstrated the value of your services, and feel that the client is ready to take the next step. Being able to read these signals correctly and act accordingly is a crucial skill.

EFFECTIVE CLOSING TECHNIQUES

1. **Direct closing:** After addressing all of the customer's concerns, ask a direct question to close the sale, such as "Can we start on the project next Monday?"
2. **Closing summary:** Summarize all the benefits and values your consultancy offers and ask if the client is ready to proceed. This reinforces the value and helps solidify the decision.
3. **Closing by alternative:** Give the customer two options that both lead to closing, such as choosing between two service packages. This limits the decision to which option to choose, and not to deciding whether to hire or not.
4. **Conditional Closing:** Use conditions to overcome last hesitations, such as "If I can adjust the schedule as you need, are you ready to start this project with us?"

OVERCOMING THE FEAR OF COMMITMENT

Many clients hesitate at the last moment due to fear of commitment. To overcome this:

- **Strengthen support and follow-up:** Assure the customer that they are not alone after signing the

contract. Highlight ongoing support and resources that will be available.
- **Minimize risk:** Offer guarantees or mention flexible cancellation policies, if applicable. Showing that you are confident enough to offer these options can help alleviate customer concerns.
- **Testimonials and success stories:** Recall success stories from other customers, especially those who were initially hesitant.

Closing the sale is both an art and a science. It requires understanding customer needs and behaviors, as well as applying closing techniques that encourage a positive decision. With practice and application of the strategies discussed, you will be able to increase your conversion rates and build a solid base of satisfied customers.

Ready to take your skills to a global context? In the next chapter, " **CULTURE AND INTERNATIONAL SALES** ", we will explore how to adapt your sales strategies to different cultures and international markets, ensuring effectiveness and respect for cultural diversities. Let's move forward to expand your market horizons?

CULTURE AND INTERNATIONAL SALES

When expanding your consulting operations into international markets, understanding and respecting cultural differences becomes crucial. This chapter focuses on how to adapt your sales strategies to effectively serve diverse cultures, ensuring that your approaches are sensitive and effective on the global stage.

THE IMPORTANCE OF CULTURAL SENSITIVITY

Cultural sensitivity is fundamental to success in the global market. It involves understanding and respecting the cultural norms, values, etiquettes and communication expectations of different countries and regions. An approach that works well in one country may not be effective or even frowned upon in another.

STRATEGIES FOR CULTURAL ADAPTATION

1. **Cultural research:** Before entering a new market, invest time and resources in understanding the cultural context. This may include studies on local business practices, communication preferences and purchasing decisions.
2. **Training and consulting:** Consider working with cultural consultants or participating in training that can prepare you and your team to interact effectively with international clients.
3. **Tailoring marketing materials:** Customize your marketing materials to reflect local language, values, and aesthetics. This shows respect for the client's culture and increases the relevance of your communication.
4. **Flexibility in Negotiations:** Be prepared to adapt your negotiation style as needed. Some cultures prefer a more direct negotiation process, while others value long-term relationships and detailed discussions before closing a deal.
5. **Using translators and interpreters:** In situations where

language barriers may be an obstacle, employing the services of translators or interpreters can help ensure that your messages are clearly understood.

LEGAL AND ETHICAL CONSIDERATIONS

- **Legal Compliance:** Ensure your operations comply with local and international laws. This includes trade regulations, employment laws and data privacy standards.
- **Business Ethics:** Maintain a high standard of ethics in all of your operations. This is especially important in international markets, where business practices can differ significantly.

COMMON CHALLENGES AND HOW TO OVERCOME THEM

- **Time Zone Differences:** Managing time zone differences requires careful planning to ensure timely and effective communications.
- **Physical distances:** Use technology to maintain regular and effective communication, and plan in-person visits when possible and necessary to strengthen relationships.

Expanding your consultancy into the international market is an exciting opportunity that requires a meticulously tailored approach. By understanding and respecting cultural differences, you can build long-lasting, successful relationships with clients around the world.

Ready to measure the success of your sales strategies? In the next chapter, " **MEASURING SUCCESS IN CONSULTING SALES** ," we'll explore methods for evaluating and optimizing your sales performance, ensuring you continue to grow and adapt effectively. Let's move forward to understand how to monitor and continually improve your sales practices?

MEASURING SUCCESS IN CONSULTING SALES

Evaluating the performance of your sales strategies is crucial to understanding what is working and what needs to be adjusted. This chapter covers methods for measuring the success of your consulting sales, allowing you to make informed adjustments and optimize your practices to achieve even better results.

ESTABLISHING SUCCESS METRICS

To effectively measure success, it is essential to define which metrics are most relevant to your business objectives. Some common metrics include:

1. **Conversion rate:** The percentage of potential customers who become paying customers. This helps you evaluate the effectiveness of your sales techniques and proposals.
2. **Average Contract Value:** The average value of contracts signed. This may indicate whether you are managing to sell more complete or higher-value solutions.
3. **Sales cycle:** The average time needed to close a contract from the first contact. Shorter cycles may indicate greater sales efficiency.
4. **Customer satisfaction:** Measured through direct feedback and satisfaction surveys. This reflects not only the quality of your service delivery, but also the success of your sales interactions.
5. **Customer Retention Rate:** Indicates how many customers continue to do business with you after the initial contract conclusion. High retention rates are a sign of high-quality customer service and satisfaction.

USING ANALYSIS TOOLS

To collect and analyze data efficiently, consider using CRM software (Customer Relationship Management), which can help track customer interactions, completed sales, and other important metrics. Digital analytics tools can also provide insights into customer behavior on your website and effectiveness of digital marketing campaigns.

ADJUSTING DATA-BASED STRATEGIES

Based on the data you collect, make adjustments to your sales strategies to address weaknesses and capitalize on areas of success. For example:

- **Refine sales approaches:** If your conversion rate is low, you may need to review your closing techniques or improve lead qualifications.
- **Adjust value proposals:** If the average contract value is lower than expected, consider adjusting your proposals to include more value or realigning your prices.
- **Improve customer support:** If customer satisfaction is not at the desired level, implement customer service improvements or provide additional training to your staff.

Measuring success in consulting sales is an ongoing process that requires constant attention to metrics and a willingness to adapt strategies as needed. By committing to rigorous and ongoing analysis, you ensure that your consulting practice not only meets market expectations, but exceeds them.

Ready to continue developing your skills? In the next chapter, " **TRAINING AND CONTINUOUS TRAINING** ", we will discuss the importance of investing in the continuous development of your skills and that of your team to maintain competitiveness in the market. Let's move forward to ensure you stay ahead in your consulting career?

TRAINING AND CONTINUOUS TRAINING

Continuous training and training are essential to maintain competitiveness and relevance in the consultancy market. This chapter addresses the importance of investing in your professional development and that of your team, exploring effective strategies to ensure that skills remain sharp and aligned with market demands.

THE IMPORTANCE OF CONTINUING EDUCATION

In the dynamic field of consulting, market demands, technologies and best practices are constantly evolving. Continuous training not only helps improve the quality of the services you offer, it also demonstrates a commitment to excellence and adapting to change, elements valued by customers.

STRATEGIES FOR CONTINUOUS DEVELOPMENT

1. **Formal training:** Invest in courses, workshops and seminars relevant to your area of specialization. This may include topics such as new technologies, advanced consulting methods, business management, or even interpersonal skills such as leadership and communication.
2. **Professional certifications:** Obtaining industry-recognized certifications can not only enhance your skills but also strengthen your credibility and attractiveness in the market.
3. **Practical learning:** Engage in projects that challenge your current skills and allow for the practical application of new knowledge and techniques.
4. **Mentoring and coaching:** Participating in mentoring programs, whether as a mentor or as a mentee, can be an excellent way to exchange knowledge, learn from the experience of others and expand your professional network.
5. **Collaborative learning:** Host team learning sessions where members share insights and knowledge about

industry trends, case studies, or innovations.

IMPLEMENTING A DEVELOPMENT PLAN

- **Needs assessment:** Regularly assess personal development needs and those of your team. Identify which skills are needed to meet current and future market demands.
- **Development planning:** Create a development plan that aligns identified needs with available training opportunities. Set clear goals and deadlines for achieving those objectives.
- **Balancing work and learning:** Organize training so that it complements, rather than compromises, your work responsibilities. This may include dedicating specific hours to learning or integrating professional development into the daily workflow.

MEASURING DEVELOPMENT IMPACT

- **Feedback and reviews:** Use customer feedback and performance reviews to measure the impact of development on work. This will help adjust the focus of training programs to maximize benefits.
- **Training ROI:** Calculate the return on investment from training activities by analyzing improvements in productivity, service quality and customer satisfaction.

Investing in capacity building and ongoing training is crucial to sustaining growth and innovation in your consulting practice. By staying educated and adaptable, you ensure that your consultancy not only survives, but thrives in a competitive environment.

Ready to explore legal and ethical aspects relevant to consultants? In the next chapter, " **LEGISLATION AND ETHICS IN CONSULTING** ", we will discuss guidance on how to navigate legal and ethical challenges within the consulting industry. Will we continue to strengthen your knowledge base and professional

REGINALDO OSNILDO

practice?

LEGISLATION AND ETHICS IN CONSULTING

Navigating the legal and ethical aspects is essential for any consultant who wants to maintain a respectable and legally sound professional practice. This chapter provides a guide to the most relevant legal and ethical considerations in consulting, helping you understand obligations and best practices for operating within legal and ethical frameworks.

UNDERSTANDING THE IMPORTANCE OF ETHICS AND LEGALITY

Ethics and legality are fundamental to building trust and credibility with customers and business partners. Maintaining high ethical standards and complying with relevant legislation not only protects you from legal risks, but also establishes a solid foundation for the sustainable growth of your consulting practice.

LEGAL ASPECTS IN CONSULTING

1. **Service contracts:** Ensure that all customer agreements are formalized in clear and comprehensive contracts. These should detail the scope of the service, payment terms, obligations of both parties and termination conditions.
2. **Intellectual property rights:** Understand the importance of protecting your intellectual property and that of your customers. This includes copyrights, trademarks and patents where applicable.
3. **Confidentiality and Privacy:** Ensure the confidentiality of customer information and comply with data privacy regulations, such as GDPR in Europe or LGPD in Brazil.
4. **Regulatory compliance:** Familiarize yourself with industry-specific regulations that may impact your clients and ensure your consultancy is compliant.

ETHICAL PRINCIPLES IN CONSULTING

1. **Integrity:** Act honestly and transparently in all

interactions with customers, colleagues and other stakeholders.
2. **Professionalism:** Maintain a high standard of professionalism in your work, including accuracy, punctuality and responsibility.
3. **Confidentiality:** Strictly protect confidential information obtained in the course of your work.
4. **Conflict of interest:** Proactively identify and manage any potential conflict of interest that could compromise your objectivity or independence.

IMPLEMENTING LEGAL AND ETHICAL PRACTICES

- **Training and awareness:** Regularly train yourself and your team on relevant legal and ethical issues. This may include training sessions, informative newsletters, and ongoing learning resources.
- **Policies and procedures:** Develop and implement clear policies and procedures for dealing with ethical and legal issues. This helps ensure consistency and compliance across the organization.
- **Legal consultation:** Maintain a relationship with legal professionals who can provide advice and assistance when needed, especially in complex or specialized areas.

Taking a proactive approach to legal and ethical issues not only minimizes risk, but also strengthens trust and respect with your clients and the broader community. By committing to ethics and legal compliance, you establish a solid foundation for the success and longevity of your consulting practice.

Ready to explore strategies to expand your consulting services? In the next chapter, " **SERVICE EXPANSION STRATEGIES** ", we will discuss how you can grow and diversify your offerings to better meet your customers' needs and explore new markets. Let's move forward to expand the scope and impact of your services?

SERVICE EXPANSION STRATEGIES

Expanding your service portfolio is an excellent way to grow in the competitive consulting market. This chapter explores effective strategies for increasing the reach of your services, better meeting your customers' needs and exploring new market opportunities.

EVALUATING EXPANSION OPPORTUNITIES

Before expanding your services, it is crucial to assess the market and identify opportunities for growth. That includes:

1. **Market analysis:** Study market trends, customer demands and competitor movements to identify areas with potential for growth.
2. **Customer feedback:** Utilize direct feedback from customers to understand their unmet needs or areas of service that require improvement or expansion.
3. **Competency Assessment:** Consider the existing competencies within your team and determine whether you can expand your services or whether additional training or hiring is needed.

STRATEGIES FOR SERVICE EXPANSION

1. **Development of new services:** Create new services that complement existing ones or that meet new identified customer needs. For example, if you offer financial consulting, you might consider expanding into strategic or risk management consulting.
2. **Partnerships and collaborations:** Form partnerships with other companies or consultants who can offer complementary skills or services. This can expand your offer without requiring a large initial investment.
3. **Vertical or horizontal specialization:** Consider specializing in certain industries (vertical) or expanding your range of services within a specific industry (horizontal). This can help differentiate your consultancy in the market.

4. **Licensing or franchising:** Explore opportunities to license your methods or services, or develop a franchising model that allows for faster expansion and lower direct operating costs.

IMPLEMENTING SERVICE EXPANSION

- **Implementation plan:** Develop a detailed plan for introducing new services, including development steps, timeline, budget, and required resources.
- **Effective Communication:** Ensure you clearly communicate the expansion of services to existing and potential customers. Use all available channels, such as email, social media, and networking events.
- **Monitoring and evaluation:** After implementation, monitor the performance of new services and collect customer feedback for ongoing adjustments.

Expanding your service offering can not only increase your revenue, but also strengthen customer relationships by providing them with a more complete solution. With careful planning and strategic execution, you can effectively increase the reach and impact of your consultancy in the market.

Ready to integrate sustainable practices into your service offering? In the next chapter, " **SUSTAINABILITY AND CONSULTING** ", we will discuss how you can incorporate environmental and social considerations into your consulting practices, aligning your services with the growing demands for corporate responsibility. Let's move forward to make your consultancy more green and socially responsible?

SUSTAINABILITY AND CONSULTING

Integrating sustainable practices into your consulting offering not only meets a growing demand for corporate responsibility, but also positions your company as a leader in conscious, ethical business practice. This chapter discusses how you can implement sustainability strategies in your consultancy, ensuring that your services not only generate profit, but also promote a positive impact on the environment and society.

THE IMPORTANCE OF SUSTAINABILITY IN CONSULTING

Sustainability has become a strategic imperative for companies of all sizes, influencing purchasing decisions and business partnerships. Furthermore, incorporating sustainable practices can help mitigate risks, innovate products and services, and build a positive reputation in the market.

STRATEGIES TO PROMOTE SUSTAINABILITY

1. **Environmental audits:** Start by performing environmental audits of your own and your customers' business processes. Identify areas where improvements can be made to reduce the ecological footprint.
2. **Sustainable Consulting Services:** Develop and deliver services that help clients implement sustainable business practices. This may include resource optimization, waste management, energy efficiency and corporate social responsibility strategies.
3. **Training and education:** Provide training to your team and customers on the importance of sustainability and how sustainable practices can be integrated into daily operations.
4. **Partnerships with sustainable organizations:** Collaborate with NGOs, academic institutions and other organizations that promote sustainability. This can expand your reach and add value to your services.
5. **Sustainable certifications:** Obtain sustainability certifications for your own company and help your

customers do the same. This not only reinforces the commitment to sustainable practices, but also serves as a competitive differentiator.

IMPLEMENTING SUSTAINABLE PRACTICES

- **Integration into value propositions:** Highlight sustainability as an integral part of value propositions for new customers. Show how sustainable practices can benefit not only the environment but also long-term business performance.
- **Sustainability reports:** Develop sustainability reports for your consultancy and assist your clients in creating theirs. This demonstrates transparency and commitment to continuous improvement.
- **Continuous innovation:** Stay up to date on new technologies and sustainable practices that can be applied in your consultancy and recommended to clients.

Adopting a sustainable approach to your consultancy offers a significant competitive advantage, aligning your company with modern expectations of responsible and conscious business. By promoting sustainable practices, you not only contribute to environmental and social well-being, but you also build a lasting legacy that transcends financial success.

Ready to conclude our journey and look to the future of consulting sales? In the next and final chapter, " **FUTURE OF CONSULTING SALES** ", we will explore emerging trends and how you can prepare for the next market evolutions. Shall we end this book with a vision for the future?

FUTURE OF CONSULTING SALES

As we wrap up this comprehensive guide to consulting sales, it's crucial to look to the future and consider the emerging trends that will shape this industry. This chapter not only reflects on what has been learned, but also outlines how you can prepare for future changes, ensuring that your consulting practice remains relevant and effective in the dynamic marketplace.

ASSESSING THE FUTURE OF CONSULTING SALES

The future of consulting sales will be influenced by several forces, including technological advances, changing client expectations and the growing importance of sustainable and responsible practices. Staying informed and adaptable will be more crucial than ever.

EMERGING TRENDS

1. **Digitization and technology:** Technology will continue to play a crucial role, with digital tools and advanced data analytics becoming essential for delivering personalized, insight-based advice.
2. **Consulting as a Service (CaaS):** Flexible, subscription-based service models may gain popularity, allowing clients to access consulting services on demand.
3. **Focus on customer experience:** Customer experience will be a key competitive differentiator. Consultants will need to create more engaging and personalized interactions to meet and exceed client expectations.
4. **Sustainability:** Demand for sustainability and corporate social responsibility consulting will likely increase as more companies seek to align their operations with global sustainability goals.
5. **Globalization:** As market barriers continue to decline, opportunities for international consulting will expand, requiring a deeper understanding of diverse business cultures and legal regulations.

PREPARING FOR THE FUTURE

- **Continuing education:** Continuously invest in your professional development and that of your team to stay ahead of trends and in-demand skills.
- **Flexibility and innovation:** Develop the ability to quickly adapt your service offerings and business models in response to market changes.
- **Network Expansion:** Continue building and nurturing your professional network, both locally and internationally, to explore new market opportunities and strategic partnerships.
- **Trend Monitoring:** Stay informed about changes in the industry through regular research, participating in forums and subscribing to relevant publications.

Throughout this book, we explore the many facets of consulting sales, from understanding the market to adapting sales strategies to different cultural contexts. As you move forward, remember that success in consulting sales is not just based on effective techniques, but also on a holistic approach that values ethics, responsibility, and an ongoing commitment to learning and innovation. Equipped with the knowledge and strategies discussed, you are now better prepared to thrive in an ever-evolving consulting world. Let's move forward together towards a bright future in consulting!

As we turn the final page of this journey together, I sincerely hope that the learnings shared here have touched your heart and sparked new perspectives. If this book has brought you any value, I kindly ask that you take a few moments to leave a review on Amazon. Your words not only help me grow and hone my craft, but they also guide other readers in their quests for knowledge and inspiration. Your opinion is a valuable gift, both for me and for the community of readers looking for stories that transform. I sincerely thank you for sharing this journey with me and I hope we can meet again in the pages of a new adventure.

REGINALDO OSNILDO

Hello, I'm Reginaldo Osnildo, author and innovator in the areas of sales, technology, and communication strategies. My experience ranges from the academic environment, as a professor and researcher at the University of Southern Santa Catarina, to practice as a strategist at Grupo Catarinense de Rádios. With a PhD in sales narratives and digital convergence, and a master's degree in storytelling and social imaginary, I bring my readers a unique fusion of theory and practice. My goal is to provide knowledge in a simple, practical and didactic language, encouraging direct application in personal and professional life.

Yours sincerely

Reginaldo Osnildo

+55 48 991913865

reginaldoosnildo@gmail.com

www.ingramcontent.com/pod-product-compliance
Lightning Source LLC
Chambersburg PA
CBHW070350230526
45471CB00006B/2497